Heart Songs

Heart Songs

Written and Illustrated by Matthew Joseph Thaddeus Stepanek
"Mattie"

VSP Books
HYPERION
New York

ISBN: 0-7868-6947-X

FIRST EDITION

10 9 8 7 6 5 4 3 2 1

Printed in the U.S.A.

CONTENTS

Dedication
This book is dedicated to those who believe
in celebrating the gifts of life every day,
especially my mom, all of my kin, and the
entire staff of the Pediatric Intensive Care
Unit at Children's National Medical Center.
Always remember to play after every storm!

Senses

5

Making Real Sense of the Senses

Our eyes are for looking at things,
But they are also for crying
When we are very happy or very sad.
Our ears are for listening,
But so are our hearts.
Our noses are for smelling food,
But also the wind and the grass and
If we try very hard, butterflies.
Our hands are for feeling,
But also for hugging and touching so gently.
Our mouths and tongues are for tasting,
But also for saying words, like
"I love you," and
"Thank you, God, for all of these things."

The Gift of Color

Thank You
For all the colors of the rainbow.
Thank You
For sharing these colors
With all of the fish
And all of the birds
And all of the flowers
That You have given us.
And thank You
For the colors of the
Heaven-in-the-earth
And of the
Heaven-in-the-sky,
And for sharing these colors
In the people of the world.
You give us color
As a gift, God,
And I thank You
For all of these
Beautiful colors and
Beautiful things and
Beautiful people.
What special gifts
You have given to us!

The Smell of a Noise

Shhhh...
I smell something.
It smells like a noise.
Like a turtle noise.
Yes, that's what it is.
It is a turtle noise,
And it is wonderful,
Because turtles
Live inside of seashells.
Would you like to
Live in a seashell?
It would smell like
A turtle noise,
But I think
It would be wonderful!

Angel-Wings

This morning,
I smelled something very good.
Perhaps,
It was a rainbow.
Or maybe,
It was a dinosaur smile.
Or even,
A seashell.
I am not sure
What I smelled.
And I am not sure
What rainbows
Or dinosaur smiles
Or seashells
Smell like.
But I'm sure they smell wonderful.
Wonderful and special
Like the smell of
Angel-Wings.
But also,
I'm sure they smell
A little sad,
Because we can't really smell
A rainbow,
Or a dinosaur smile,
Or a seashell,
Or especially,
We can't really smell
The wonderful smell
Of Angel-Wings.

Very Special Candy

One day,
I will make a bag of
Very Special Candy.
The candy will come in
All different colors,
Colors like you see in
Good Ordinary Candy.
But...
The flavors will be
So different and
So special and
So wonderful.
There will be little
Blue candies
That taste like sky.
And the little
Green and brown candies
Will taste like grass and trees.
The orange ones
Will taste like butterfly,
The yellow ones
Like flowers and sunshine,
And the white ones
Like clouds in Heaven.
And then,
I will make a very, very
Special piece of candy,
That is all different colors
And that glows like a halo.
And that will be the one
That tastes like
Rainbow and Angels.

When My Feet Itch

When my feet itch,
Maybe I'll think about
Riding on a dinosaur
With my mom —
And then,
I won't remember that my feet itch.
When my feet itch,
Maybe I'll think about
Spending the night at the
North Pole with Santa Claus —
And then,
It will be too cold for my feet to itch.
When my feet itch,
Maybe I'll think about
Playing with Nick and Ben
Because they're some of the
Best friends a kid could ever have —
And then,
I won't care if my feet itch or not.
Or maybe, when my feet itch,
I'll think about Angels —
Because they don't make
You itch when you touch them.

Seasons 12

Leaf for a Day

Today,
I think I will be a tree.
Or perhaps,
A leaf on a branch on the tree.
I will feel
The gentle breeze,
And then I will
`Plip' off of my branch and my tree
And float in the wind.
I will go
Back and forth in the breeze
All the way down to the ground.
And after I rest
And say `hello'
To the grass and dirt and bugs,
I will call to the wind,
`Come and take me
To visit my other leaf-friends
On all of the other trees, please.'
And the gentle breeze
Will come
And pick me up
So that I can jump and dance
With all of the other
Tree-stars and tree-flowers
That God gave the world.
What a special idea
To be, today.

On the Mountain of Tree-Stars

Summer is almost over.
Soon, it will be September,
And then, it will be fall.
And when it is fall,
We can play with all
The tree-stars that fall
To us from up high.
And when the tree-stars fall
From the sky,
We can build a leaf-mountain.
First, when all
The leaves fall
From the sky,
We put them all
Together into a mountain-pile
Way up high.
Then, we get a string and tie
Them all
Together so that when
The wind blows they won't fly
Away from the mountain-pile.
And last, we climb
Up the leaf-mountain,
And we stand up so high
Next to the sky,
And then —- sliiiiiiide —-
We slide
Aaaaaaaaalll
The way to the bottom of the mountain-leaf pile.
So when the fall
Comes it will get chilly,
And things will start to fall
Like the season.
But they don't fall
With a boom!
Only they fall
Like a floating leaf, or
Like a little boy on
The Mountain of Tree-Stars.

Winter Luck

Snowflakes...
They come down so slow,
And sometimes so fast,
Looking like pretty stars
Falling down, down, down
To the ground.
Little stars with little holes,
Bigger stars with bigger holes,
They are all cuddly snowflake stars.
Snowflakes of the tiny snows,
Snowstars of the bigger snows,
I will catch you on my hand
Or on my tongue
And make a wish...
I will make a wish on
My falling snowstar,
And then have good luck
All day, all night, all Ever.

Important Things

When I grow up,
I think maybe
I will be a snowman,
Because when it
Snows outside,
I'll already be cold
And like it.
And children will
Play with me,
And laugh
And sing
And dance
All around me.
And those are important
Things to have happen
When you grow up.

Indian Winter

Hey!
It's cold out here today!
This is May,
And it's supposed to be
Spring
Turning into
Summer,
So I can have my birthday.
But I need my jacket,
And my hat.
Oh, bother!
I wonder —-
Who played with the seasons
Last night
While we were all sleeping?

The Eye of the Beholder

Dandelions are NOT weeds!
See?
They have beautiful
Yellow flowers on them.
They have lovely
Green stems.
Mommy puts them
In a jar of water
In the kitchen —-
They are flowers!
See?
They are round.
They are round and yellow.
Oh, mommy,
Please tell him
He's making a big mistake!
Poor little dandelions...
He's pulling them all up
And calling them "weeds."
Oh, this is
So horrible, so sad!
What would God say if
He saw you sending all of these
Poor, little, round, yellow
Dandelion-flowers
Back to the Lord?

Summer 'Rememberies'

After everyone has
A smoky cookout at Chip's house,
And the grown-ups make
Music on their guitars for singing and dancing,
And the children take
Off their shoes and run
Around the backyard catching
Lightning bugs in the dark —-
Then, it is a very good time to be
Happy.
And that `then' is
A very good time and
A very good feeling to remember
Ever-after.

Celebrations 20

The Importance of Windows

Windows are very good things to have.
They let you look out,
And see all the different things.
And they let you look in,
To see all the other different things.
And do you know what is the most
Special window of all?
The window in your heart,
That's between the Heaven-in-the-earth,
And the Heaven-in-the-sky.

Circle of Happiness

I am a little kid
For you to love.
I am a little kid
For you to hug and kiss.
I am a little kid
For you to say,
"You are so special,
Yes you are" to.
I am a little kid
For all of those things
And more.
And when you
Feel and say and do
All of those things,
I will be a little kid
Who will love you.
I will be a little kid
Who will hug and kiss you.
I will be a little kid
Who will say to you,
"You are so special, too,
Yes you are."
I will be a little kid
Who will do all of those things
And more.
And that is what
Happiness
Is all about.

On Being Thankful

Dear God,
I was going to thank You tonight
For a beautiful sunrise,
That was pink behind the fog down the hill,
And for a wonderful rainbow,
That I ran under pointing to
All my favorite colors,
And for such a great sunset,
That sparkled orange across the water.
I was going to thank You tonight
For all of these special gifts,
Except that none of them happened.
But do You know what?
I still love You, God,
And I have lots of other things
That I can thank You for tonight,
Even if you didn't give those
Very special gifts to me today.
It's okay, God,
Because I'll look for them all again,
When my tomorrow comes.
Amen.

Pinch of Peace

Dear God,
Tonight my prayers are for the world.
We have to stop this fighting.
We have to stop the wars.
People need to lay down their weapons,
And find peace in their hearts.
People need to stop arguing and hating.
People need to notice the good things.
People need to remember You, God.
Maybe You could come and
Shoot a little bow-and-arrow pinch
Into all the angry peoples' hearts, God.
Then they would feel You again.
And then they would realize what
They are doing and how horrible the
Killing and hating and fighting is,
And they might even begin to pray.
Then, they could reach in, and
Pull the little bow-and-arrow pinch
Out of their hearts and feel good
And be loving and living people again.
And then,
The world would be at peace, and
The children would be safe, and
The people would be happy, and
We could all say "thank You" together.
Amen.

Heartsong

I have a song, deep in my heart,
And only I can hear it.
If I close my eyes and sit very still
It is so easy to listen to my song.
When my eyes are open and
I am so busy and moving and busy,
If I take time and listen very hard,
I can still hear my Heartsong.
It makes me feel happy.
Happier than ever.
Happier than everywhere
And everything and everyone
In the whole wide world.
Happy like thinking about
Going to Heaven when I die.
My Heartsong sounds like this —-
    I love you! I love you!
    How happy you can be!
    How happy you can make
    This whole world be!
And sometimes it's other
Tunes and words, too,
But it always sings the
Same special feeling to me.
It makes me think of
Jamie, and Katie and Stevie,
And other wonderful things.
This is my special song.
But do you know what?
All people have a special song
Inside their hearts!
Everyone in the whole wide world
Has a special Heartsong.
If you believe in magical, musical hearts,
And if you believe you can be happy,
Then you, too, will hear your song.

25

The Daily Gift

You know what?
Tomorrow is a new day.
And today is a new day.
Actually,
Every day is a new day.
Thank You, God,
For all of these
Special and new days.

Special Section—
Eight Additional Poems

Barney-Muffins

Good morning!
It's a smiley-face morning.
Mommy made banana-muffins,
Because it's Stevie's birthday.
I had banana-muffins before,
At Sandy's house.
They were very, very good.
Mommy said these banana-muffins
Taste good, too,
But they are not Real
Because she didn't scratch them,
Like Sandy did.
Hey...
Are these plastic banana-muffins?
I guess we'll just have to
Use our imaginations,
And pretend.

Magical Big-Boy Underpants

Some of my big-boy underpants
Have Mickey Mouse on them.
Some of my big-boy underpants
Have Barney on them.
But some of my big-boy underpants
Are just white.
Maybe, the white underpants
Could be like
The trees in the fall,
And turn into colors.
They could change into orange
And red and yellow.
And they would be beautiful,
And very special,
And I would wear them and
Be very happy.
Except I wouldn't be happy
If they fell down,
Like the leaves do,
Onto the ground.
Then, I would get cold,
And I might trip and
Fall down, too.

Morning Shoes

Listen...
Listen carefully to the people
When they are walking to work,
Or to school, or to play,
Or even to wherever,
And the shoes can tell you what
Kind of breakfast cereal their people eat.
The ladies hurrying in pointy high-heels eat
   Coco-coco-coco-poppin'
   Coco-coco-coco-poppin'...
The men with boots and heavy steps eat
   Crunchabooma-crunchabooma-
   Crunchabooma-crunchabooma...
The teenagers who forget to tie their sneakers eat
   Sugar-chewy-munchy-boomy
   Sugar-chewy-munchy-boomy...
The children in sandals and Velcro shoes eat
   Twinkle-crinkle-marshmallow sprinkle,
   Twinkle-crinkle-marshmallow sprinkle...
And the old man in his bedroom slippers at the bus stop eats
   Snap-crackle-rustle pop,
   Snap-crackle-rustle pop...
But the babies in their strollers with little soft shoes
That have no dirt marks on the bottoms of them
Don't make any noise at all...
That's because they eat oatmeal,
And listen to hear what the grown-ups eat
So they know what to ask for when they get older.

Where the Earth Stops

Do you know where the earth stops
And it's the end of it?
It can be when you come to water,
But not usually.
Do you know why?
Because if you go out of earth
And you don't have a rocket ship
With you and you're not driving one,
You will come to the end of the earth
When you go into space.
It will be a long way,
But you can make it.
Have fun on your trip,
Bye!

The Storm

There is a big storm coming.
It is way up in the air,
Above the clouds.
It is out in space.
Maybe my friends and I
Will get into a rocket ship
And fly up into space
To see the storm.
We will look down at the storm.
When the storm is all through,
We will come back down to earth.
We will be dry, not wet,
Because we were above the storm clouds.
But it will take a long time
To fly up into that space.
So maybe,
If it is snack time,
Perhaps we will just use
An umbrella to stay dry instead.

Evening Thought

When it is getting
To be nighttime,
But it is
Not dark yet,
The farm animals
Begin to get very tired.
They need to go
Into their barns,
And inside their stables,
And inside their hutches,
And homes,
So that when
The pink and gray sunset
Is all finished,
They can go
Right to sleep,
And have
Pleasant dreams.

Scrub-a-Dub

Help, help!
All I did was take a bath!
A long bubble bath.
I washed my face,
And my hands and my feet.
I played with my mermaid,
And my whale and my boat.
And now,
Now I have
Raisin-fingers and raisin-toes!
Oh no!
Help, help!
I guess I better
Get back into the bathtub,
And wash away these
Raisin-hands and raisin-feet!
And since I am in there,
I guess I better
Just play some more,
Don't you know?

Night-Light Magic

Last night,
My mommy forgot
To turn on my night-light.
I was scared,
So I called her.
Mommy turned on the light,
And then she kissed me,
And tucked me in again.
And then,
I was a golden head in the night.
That is when I'm a little boy,
Between an Angel,
And a Wild Thing.

Index

The publishers wish to acknowledge the assis-
tance and support of the following people in the pro-
duction of this book: Martha Shaw Whitley, our amaz-
ing sister, for organizing and coordinating the people
and events which allow Mattie's book to be shared far
and wide; Marissa L. Garis, public relations and market-
ing specialist at Children's National Medical Center for
introducing us to Mattie and his mom, Jeni, and giving
us the opportunity to publish Mattie's poems; Catherine
Morrison, our production director, who tries to keep us
all organized; and Jeni Stepanek, Mattie's mom, whose
hidden talents as an editor are greatly appreciated.

Peter and Cheryl Barnes
VSP Books
Alexandria, Virginia
June 2001

Write Your Own
Heartsongs

Write Your Own
Heartsongs

Write Your Own Heartsongs

Write Your Own
Heartsongs